EXPOSING SHAME

Forever Grateful,
Johnson Mangrum

EXPOSING SHAME

Sabrina A. Mangrum

AGD PUBLISHING

EXPOSING SHAME
Copyright 2020 Sabrina A. Mangrum
Published by AGD Publishing Company

Unless otherwise indicated, Bible quotations are taken from The King James Version.

Printed in the United States of America

Paperback: 978-1-7346758-3-2
eBook: 978-1-7346758-4-9

CONTENTS

ACKNOWLEDGEMENTS

This book represents a major milestone in my journey. There have been so many extraordinary people who have greatly impacted my spiritual development. I am not able to list each of you but with a sincere heart I love you and thank you!

I want to thank the members of the Cornerstone Peaceful Bible Baptist Church, where I have served for over three decades. They are an exceptional group of people who have ministered to me as much as I have ministered to them. It is out of this exchange many revelations from God have come my way.

A special shout out to the Women of Rare Distinction® (W.O.R.D.) which is the Women's

Ministry I founded over 30 years ago. It has been a joy to share your victories as we have worked together over the years. Ladies, my love for each of you is immeasurable!

I am grateful to my husband, Daniel T. Mangrum, of almost 40 years. Thank you for being YOU. Your support, advice, wit, and genuine love have been instrumental in my evolving to be the woman I am today. I am forever grateful.

To my wonderful daughters Danielle Sabrina and Diamond Shekinah, my precious gifts from God, I would like to thank you for your prayers and words of encouragement. Both of which were indeed very instrumental in making sure I stayed focused and completed this assignment. I love you. (Philippians 4:13).

I am very thankful and wish to acknowledge the assistance and support received from Allison G. Daniels' AGD Publishing Company and her team;

I am forever grateful to them in helping to get this project to print.

Most importantly, I want to thank God, who saw fit to call me into the ministry and entrust me with the lives of His precious people. I hope this book is a blessing to those who read it. I pray that it will facilitate deliverance and healing from the affliction of shame.

CHAPTER ONE

Identifying Your Shame

"For your shame ye shall have double; and for confusion they shall rejoice in their portion: therefore in their land they shall possess the double: everlasting joy shall be unto them." (Isaiah 61:7)

There is not a more tragic event in the history of Israel than its fall to the Babylonian Empire. The defeat at the hand of this foreign invader caused deep disappointment and uncertainty. This was something hard for them to fathom. Their theology was based on Jehovah being the Almighty God. They believed in a God who was sovereign and all-powerful. It was difficult for them to process how with God being on their side, they had been overrun by a heathen nation. They were clearly warned that this could happen from the many prophets, including Isaiah, if they did not repent. But somehow when it happened, they were in total disbelief. To absorb this great loss was traumatic and heart-wrenching. Aside from the apparent material loss and physical destruction, there was the additional embarrassment associated with it. The mental pain was deep and impactful. They had always seen themselves as God's chosen people. They enjoyed a status where they considered themselves the apple of God's eye. Their identity was tied to them being the ones God held in a special light. The Babylonians conquering them, and the subsequent captivity clouded this long-standing belief about themselves. There was an element where their sense of well-being took a major hit. Beyond the loss of their political independence as a nation, there was the humiliation of being laid low. The Scripture, Isaiah 61:7, specifically addresses this sense of shame. Isaiah, the Prophet, describes how God is going to minister to the condition of their minds that resulted from the loss; that is, the way this made them feel inside and the way all of this left much damage to the way they felt about themselves. Isaiah promises they will receive double blessings for the shame they experienced. They would also be vindicated for the confusion hurled against them. Confusion is defined in **The New Strong's Exhaustive Concordance of the Bible** as dishonor, reproach, or disgrace. The land they will possess will be double that of what had been taken from them. Most of all, they will have everlasting joy in contrast to their extreme sadness. The narrative would be changed for them. Beyond improvement of the situation, God was going to do a work in which He was going to eliminate the effect of all they had been through. It was imperative that as much as they needed to address their loss as a nation, they also needed to address their need to be healed from the shame of it all. The two go hand in hand.

Healing means to exact a cure or make whole. It relates to the act of restoring to health. This act of healing is holistic: spirit, soul, and body. There is the healing of your heart which addresses a wounded spirit or broken heart and the healing of your soul which addresses transforming the way you think, feel and your desires. Third, healing for your physical body is necessary to address the physical manifestations of sicknesses and diseases that are linked to inner distress.

The assumption made is that when you suffer loss, you not only experience the disappointment of the material loss, but your inward man is wounded as well. When things happened to you, it left behind a degree of damage or injury. On the surface, you might only desire to regain what was lost, but God does a work in the healing of your inner man. The aim is that you can experience complete deliverance and healing.

Getting back the things you had before, without dealing with the inner hurt you experienced from losing them in the first place, is an incomplete restoration. Healing your inner man equips you to appreciate the recovery and restoration of your former things. Oftentimes, while you might experience relief and even rejoice because you got back what you lost, on the inside, you are not healed. The release and joy cannot last because it is prone to resurface.

God wants to bless you in a way where the restoration goes deeper than the surface. He wants to bless you in a way where He can address the negative impression left by the experiences. There were some things which impacted you in a way where they generated certain fears in you. Because of having gone through those things you became angry and resentful. Sometimes, these experiences caused you to feel negative emotions like guilt, insecurity, and bitterness.

A bad experience has impacted your memory in such a way that any time you encounter anything associated with what you have been through, you experience discomfort and pain. Like a video being replayed, the negative and painful vibes from what happened reappears. It is relived all over again. This can weaken your faith. It can cause you to anticipate a bad result. It can cause you to literally brace yourself as if you will have another bad experience. Long after something happened, you can still feel guilt over something you did. Long after something took place, you can still feel angry over what someone did to you. The pain of what someone said ten years ago can still sting you.

Experiencing certain things triggers memories that make you realize that while the incident happened a long time ago, it is very much alive in how it still affects you. You still have strong emotions regarding what happened. You had no idea it was still in you. It could be attending a funeral of a loved one or what you experienced at a gravesite. It could be an encounter with an old friend. It can happen when you go home and see the old house. It can be when you flip through an album and see an old picture: suddenly the flood of emotions will arise. Certain people, places, or things can trigger traumatic experiences from your past.

It was the embarrassment and humiliation of what happened. It was the indignity of it. There is a corresponding emotion associated with the loss of something which dictates how you feel about yourself. You were traumatized and this changed your thinking. It affects how you view yourself. It affects how you view life. Because of this experience your self-hood, your self-image and even your sense of identity were exposed in a negative way. It was disgraceful. It was demeaning. You looked bad. You were the object of ridicule.

There are some bad experiences that carry with them a stigma and an added aura of shame. Several things made this experience especially hurtful for the children of Israel. It was compounded with the fact that everyone saw their fall. It was public!

QUESTIONS FOR YOU:

What thoughts ran through your mind as you pondered

identifying your shame?

_____

_____

_____

_____

_____

_____

_____

Trigger Points?

_____

_____

_____

_____

_____

_____

_____

_____

_____

_____

_____

_____

_____

_____

_____

_____

_____

_____

_____

_____

_____

_____

Noted herein are types of shame we live with each and every day. It is in no way an exhaustive list:

YOU ARE NOT ALONE!!

- Past failures, mistakes, lies, cheating, bankruptcy, being fired, divorce, DUI's, negative words that have been spoken over you (parents, employers, teachers, pastors...), had a child and you were not married at the time, you were born out of wedlock.

- Incarceration, criminal records, abuse(s), addiction(s), poverty, bad habits.

- Didn't go to college, dropped out of school, expelled from school.

- Abortion, paid for an abortion, miscarriage, fornication, STD's, AIDs, adultery, prostitution, pornography.

- Rape, molestation, abandonment,

rejection, losses, betrayal.

- Physical appearance, body-shame, sexuality, sexism, colorism, and racism.

QUESTION FOR YOU:

How has any of the above impacted your life?

_____

_____

_____

_____

_____

_____

_____

_____

_____

_____

_____

_____

_____

Journaling My Thoughts

SHAME:
THE VICTIM MINDSET THAT'S ASSOCIATED
WITH BONDAGE AND LIES

MY NAME IS SHAME.

MY VICTIMS ARE MANY.

I CAUSE YOU TO

DUMMY DOWN, HIDE, BACK DOWN,

SHRINK, GIVE IN, GIVE UP, AND THROW IN

THE TOWEL, TO ACT COWARDLY.

I GUIDE YOU AWAY FROM YOUR

GOD-GIVEN POTENTIAL.

YES, GOD DID HAVE A PLAN,

BUT BEING THE BULLY THAT I AM,

I INTERCEPTED HIS PLAN

FOR MY PURPOSE, MY GLORY AND MY HONOR.

YES, I AM A DECEIVER.

I THRIVE, BASED ON LIES AND WRONG ASSUMPTIONS. I AM

ALWAYS LURKING

BEHIND, BETWEEN, BENEATH.

SHAME GIVES THE ASSUMPTION THAT THIS IS AS FAR

AS YOU CAN GO,

THAT YOU WILL NEVER MEASURE UP.

YOU WILL NEVER FIT IN.

SHAME SAYS: THAT'S NOT FOR US –THAT'S FOR THEM.

LIMITING, RESTRICTING, BINDING – YES, THAT'S

ME (SHAME)

I COME IN MANY DISGUISES.

I THRIVE IN DARKNESS,

AND I AM BOLD AS I CAN BE.

NO NEED FOR YOU TO RUFFLE ANY
FEATHERS.

LET'S KEEP OUR RELATIONSHIP A SECRET.

DON'T TELL –NO, DON'T SAY A WORD.

WE'VE COME THIS FAR... RIGHT?

WHATEVER YOU DO, DON'T TELL.

TRUST ME (SHAME says) YOUR SECRET IS SAFE
WITH ME,

BECAUSE IT IS IN THE DARK PLACE

WHERE I, Shame, PREVAIL.

Penned by Sabrina A. Mangrum

CHAPTER TWO

The Power of Shame

Herein, for the purpose of this book, let me share a definition of what is meant by shame. Shame is the negative, painful, toxic thoughts you have within yourself about yourself! As it says in Proverbs 23:7, "...as a man thinketh in his heart so is he." These thoughts are limiting in that they inhibit you from thinking freely. They cause you to experience a sense of uneasiness about yourself. There is a feeling of being ashamed and not measuring up in terms of value or worth. Confidence becomes hard to come by. Peace is difficult to attain.

Boldness is suppressed. Worst of all, the mind cannot be at ease.

Many Christians suffer from the effects of shame. Despite having been saved and forgiven by the blood of Jesus, shame continues to exercise its influence in their lives. I thought it was necessary to expose it so that liberty can take place.

In the Gospel of Luke 3:15-17, NKJV, Luke reports: "Now as the people were in expectation, and all reasoned in their hearts about John, whether he was the Christ or not, John answered, saying to all, "I indeed baptize you with water; but One mightier than I is coming, whose sandal strap I am not worthy to loose. He will baptize you with the Holy Spirit and fire. His winnowing fan is in His hand, and He will thoroughly clean out His threshing floor, and gather the wheat into His barn; but the chaff He will burn with unquenchable fire."

This is comparable to an agricultural practice that

takes place in many ancient cultures known as winnowing. It is the process that separates the wheat from the chaff. The same way wheat goes through a process of separating the worthless chaff from the edible grain. The work of the Holy Spirit is to take us through a process in which He removes our chaff. The Holy Spirit works in us to remove the chaff that can hinder us from reaching our full potential and fulfilling our purpose. Much like the separation process for wheat, there can be serious inappropriate and damaging elements inside us. So often, shame has been one of the foremost types of chaff that has been quite problematic in its ability to keep people stuck. Shame can be the result of current events or it can be a carryover from our lives before Christ. It can hang on even though we are now saved from our sins.

Sanctification is when a believer is being changed from their old Adamic Nature to the nature of Jesus

Christ. These things have attached themselves to us through life's experiences. In this process we are confronted with strongholds or certain mindsets that can be quite limiting. Our life experiences can affect us. What people say over us can shape what we believe about ourselves. Words are powerful. What a person says to us can go deep into our inner being. Your confidence and sense of self-worth can be affected by the words spoken over you. The Holy Spirit will do a sanctifying work to expose those types of things operating inside you. First, the Holy Spirit will cleanse and separate anything that is not fruitful and beneficial to you. Secondly, He will then give you the divine ability to do the things shame prevented you from being able to do. Third, the Holy Spirit will continue to assist you in maintaining your freedom as you continue to grow in the relationship with Him. As Jesus says, in John 8:31, "If ye continue in my word, then are ye my disciples." Sanctification exposes wrong assumptions we have about ourselves. It was not until I began to be a student of the Bible that I came to realize my deficiency. As Paul said to Timothy, **"Study to shew thyself approved unto God, a workman that needeth not to be ashamed, rightly dividing the word of truth."** (2Timothy 2:15) Who I was and who I was claiming to be were total opposites. I was claiming boldness, confidence, favor, and faith. However, my reality was fear, timidity, rejection, and shame. I tried unsuccessfully to do better, be better, and act better but to no avail. I needed a power greater than myself. That is why by God's grace and mercy He has sent us the Holy Spirit to help us. It is very important that if you want wholeness and freedom you have to be open and honest about who you were (past), who you are (present) and who you want to become (future). The Holy Spirit began to reveal to me that I had suppressed a lot of hurt and pain in my life because of Shame. My experiences had caused me to be extremely shy and fearful, so I actually thought this was normal. After all, that's what I saw with many of my family members. I assumed this was the way I was supposed to be. This was my personality. I had to be like this because it was who I was. We need to be aware of the fact that we are shaped by our environment. We are influenced greatly by our life experiences. However, the word of God says in 2 Timothy, 1:7, **"For God has not given us a spirit of fear, but of power and of love and of a sound mind."** Sanctification is like the layers of an onion being pulled back. As that layer was exposed, I realized I had accepted lies based on flawed assumptions regarding my birth. Those assumptions led me to believe that life was going to be hard and difficult. As The Holy Spirit eradicates and brings to light your experiences you get clarity on why you are the person you are. What you experienced has caused you to be a certain type of person. For every cause, there is an effect. What you experienced does not have to label you as a certain type of person anymore. Please allow the Holy Spirit to separate the two. Allow Him to cleanse what you feel is dirty, painful, and broken. As you surrender a transformation will begin to take place.

Shame is something that can fly under the radar. It can go undetected. It might be affecting you, even now, and you are not aware of it. Sanctification may feel uncomfortable, but it is necessary to come to grips with those things planted in your heart. Things like disgrace and humiliation. There is a need for sanctification so that you can be delivered and experience freedom.

The winnowing process requires the wheat to be tossed into the air so that the heavily valuable grain can fall to the ground, and then the chaff can be blown away.

The wheat is then collected and set apart for future use. Likewise the sanctification process exposes the light on the shame (chaff) in our minds, and brings liberation, and releases us with a new capacity to fulfill our Kingdom of God assignments!

As stated previously, SHAME is a type of chaff; its goal is to keep you from your true identity. It is associated with the word ashamed which is to be embarrassed because of one's actions, characteristics, or associations. It can have a profound effect on you. For example, you can be reluctant to do something through fear of the indignity and disparagement. It can literally control you. It can dictate to you what you will do or not do. Depending on how deep it is, it can literally take over your personality. It can change you completely. Shame can change an outgoing, confident person to a nervous, withdrawn person.

The nature of shame makes it something that is inherently unpleasant. It can make you sensitive. It can affect how you relate to people. It can conger up feelings of regret and disappointment inside you. Often shame is simply pushed down into our subconscious mind. When we encounter someone or something that may remind us of it a certain reaction is triggered. We may cry or experience anxiety, but nothing is done about it. Over time you can assume it is just something you have to live with. It is something you compensate for. You can even develop coping mechanisms wherein you learn how to avoid anything that remotely reminds you of the experience. You can also develop elaborate defensive strategies to ensure you don't get involved in a situation where you might encounter it again. For example, certain people are totally off limits. Certain places associated with what happened are places you never visit. Even certain things you may have done in the past, because of their association with the shame, are things you never do anymore. It is like you have a house where there are certain rooms you never go in again because you want to avoid the shame associated in your mind with that room.

This can go on for such a long time in that you are not even aware of how pervasive the spirit of shame is in your life. Over time you can learn to live with it. You might even assume its effects are normal. You come up with justifications for it. For example, you assume things are the way they are as part of your personality. You believe you are THIS kind of person. You think these are the only things you like to do. You may believe you are not good at certain things; not even realizing these things are the effects of shame. These things are bringing bondage to you. Viewing yourself in this manner inhibits or hinders you from being free to live the life God intended for you.

The reason this is so important is that shame represents the effect of a bad experience you may have had. You can be far removed from the experience but the effects of it may continue to impact you. You assume, because something happened a long time ago, that it is over. Although some people believe and say that time heals, my belief is that time does not heal. Something that happened long ago can leave behind the effect of shame. You can still be afflicted by something from your childhood. Although many years may have passed, it can still be fresh on your mind, like it happened moments ago.

That is the power of shame. Unchecked it can become engrained. It can feed off itself and like cancer in your physical body, grow into something deadly. Shame is serious. If it is not addressed, it continues to wreak havoc in your inner being. When you think about the interrelationship between stresses in destroying your immune system, you realize the danger of unaddressed shame. Shame could be the cause of developing disease and sickness in your body. It can affect your mental health. It can even impact your capacity to relate to God thereby destroying your spiritual well-being.

Nothing is more dangerous than the things you suppress. Anything that may develop, i.e., symptoms of disease, adversarial health concerns, has the potential to become very problematic; even fatal for you. Shame is one thing that can be lurking inside you doing severe damage. You may not realize it but shame is behind many decisions you make. For example, shame can make you afraid to pursue certain career fields or goals. It can cause you to be afraid to go further in your education or pursue relationships with others. It can cause you to be withdrawn or an introvert. The prospect of challenges can cause you to be especially stressed out because there is energy generated from the shame inside you.

Shame can even travel in the bloodline. It can be handed down through generations and it can, literally, exist as a familiar spirit. A mother can hand it down to her daughter and her daughter can hand it down to her daughter. And so, the cycle continues in that the shame your parents encountered or experienced is something you now deal with. The shame your parents may have experienced has caused them to treat or condition you to live a specific way. That conditioning causes the shame to be passed on to you. Just like fears can be handed down to children from the fears their parents had, shame can follow that same course.

You can be oblivious that shame has literally shaped your life. Growing up in a family that had shame is all you have ever known. You don't even see shame as something foreign. You might even think shame is normal. All the corresponding behaviors associated with shame are things you think are the way you are supposed to be. You think you are supposed to be shy. You are supposed to have low self-esteem. You are supposed to lack confidence. These symptoms of shame go unchallenged because you thought nothing was wrong with the way you felt, or the way you are.

On this journey, however, pain is unmistakable. Pain indicates that something is wrong. You cannot deny that you feel pain. Shame is painful, and if nothing else, shame causes you to recognize that you have a problem. It is solace and relief that will make you want to seek help. You feel trapped when you cannot do something you know you should be able to do. There is an inherent pain you feel when you realize that you feel uncomfortable on the inside about things you should not feel uncomfortable about.

I remember talking with a young bride having difficulty relating sexually with her new husband. As a child she had been sexually molested by her uncle. Even though it happened a long time ago, there was shame still in her from the incident. Even though she deeply loved her husband, there was a blockage in her ability to relate to her husband because the shame made her feel like sex was dirty or improper. Shame can, in fact, be *on* your mind as well as *in* your mind and it can take one or several triggers to rear its ugly head again.

In another case, a mother relayed how she had such difficulty relating to her young daughter. The mother had become a mother as a teenager, and when she became pregnant, she received negative comments and treatments from her family. It wasn't until her daughter was a teenager that many of those suppressed negative feelings of rejection and shame impacted how she related to her daughter. She had to come to grips with the shame inside her mind.

There are many encounters that carry a social

stigma with them. There are experiences and encounters that a person can have that go way deeper than the outward act. Those specific encounters can essentially brand the person's identity. It is embarrassing to have been the victim of abuse or addiction. Even though you were innocent, shame attaches itself to your mind. Somehow it gets twisted and the person carries the pain of shame.

In 2008 many people got caught up in predatory mortgage lending during the recession. Millions of people were affected by companies who took advantage of people with these so-called low-interest schemes that caused many people to lose their homes. I've spoken with many victims who still carry the shame of feeling like they had let their family down. Even though it happened many years ago, and they now have beautiful homes, they struggle with the shame and the disappointment of what happened in the past.

In so many instances in talking to children in homes where the parents divorced, somehow the children think it was their fault. They carry the shame of their parents breaking up as if they had something to do with it. When the parents try to get them to take sides it further complicates the problem. It is so irrational. But shame can be irrational. It can have no rational basis and yet still exist in the minds of people.

Shame's power over me was so strong that it took years for me to accept the truth that I, Sabrina Antoinette Jefferson Lloyd Mangrum, was chosen; favored, and loved by God. I was not a mistake! I had carried the shame of being born out of wedlock as well as the guilt of believing I had ruined my beautiful mom's life. *I struggled with surely*, if it were not for me she would have been much better off! Also, the shame and rejection I experienced from my father who was too preoccupied with his own life to take any interest in mine. His absence made me question my worth for far too many years.

The main reason why I wanted to write this book was so that we can talk about this. When this comes out into the open, there is an opportunity for shame to be exposed to just how false it can be. It is something that does not have to continue to exist inside you anymore. It is time for you to be free from the mistakes and mishaps of the past. It is time for you to no longer feel the pain of shame from experiences you suffered a long time ago or even a week ago. It is time for you to move beyond your comfort zones. It is your time!

QUESTION FOR YOU:

How has the power of shame impacted your life?

_____

_____

_____

_____

_____

_____

_____

_____

_____

_____

_____

Journaling My Thoughts

CHAPTER THREE

Finding Your True Identity and Changing
Your Narratives

Shame unfortunately, is something you can find yourself living with. It is something that literally weighs you down. It is the source of ongoing turmoil inside. It is equated to a nagging pain you can feel physically because it haunts you and hangs over you. Shame makes it hard to feel secure because it sends off a message inside which suggests that you are undesirable and unattractive. It is as if you expect to be rejected because shame makes you assume people see you in a bad light. It's like a person is walking around with a neon billboard sign around their neck.

On the sign is their shame written on it. Shame makes you believe everyone can see what was said or done. That is simply not true. Do not permit shame to shut you down. One of the deceptive elements of shame is that it can exist in your life and you can appear to be unaffected by it at all. It does not stop you from getting married, having children or even a career. But the problem with shame is that it goes along with you like extra baggage and additional weight.

Shame is a more severe problem whenever you have any life experiences that are stressful and demanding. Having shame in your existence is something you work around, in addition to whatever you are dealing with. It is as if you must consume precious time and energy with it. Shame inhibits you by adding more to whatever you are dealing with. Sometimes you can't recognize it because you don't experience its effect until you are in the middle of something intense. You learn *of it* as you seek to navigate through a crisis. When dealing with a disappointment or several, shame suddenly flares up inside you. You feel additional stress and weight that is added to the situations you face. Greater fatigue is because you are fighting on two fronts. The situations itself and the shame inside you is the problem.

Shame often has a partner in guilt. Usually where you find guilt, shame is also present. It is difficult to separate the two because they are so deeply intertwined. However, they are different in that guilt is based on something you have caused or done toward others, while shame is the negative emotion you feel about yourself. When we normally address shame, we focus on its impact on our identity. Shame is the worst part of being guilty. Nothing is more disheartening than feeling shame because of being guilty. One of the amazing aspects of shame is that sometimes you can feel guilt and it can be completely a product of what is in your head. In other words, you really did not do anything but because you were accused or blamed by others or even yourself, you have shame inside you. You feel responsible for things you did not have anything to do with. You take on the pain of others when you had no role in their offense.

Shame can cause your physical body to malfunction whenever you experience guilt. As is evidenced by the man with the palsy in Matthew 9 and Luke 5, Jesus showed us there is a direct link between this man's guilt and his affliction of palsy. When Jesus addressed his need for forgiveness, the ailment was immediately healed. I dare say that shame bears down on your mind causing your physical body to literally malfunction. Many ailments and diseases people have working inside their body results from the presence of guilt and the corresponding shame.

There is a reason Jesus died for our sins. Of all the things Jesus did for us, nothing is more significant than the provision He made for our sins. When we take on the characteristics of Christ –our abiding in Him –we are forgiven; so there is no need to take on or accept shame in our lives any longer. Jesus Christ has eliminated the basis or root for guilt and shame. To believe in all Jesus did for us is to eradicate any reason to carry guilt and shame. To live with shame is to believe something other than what God's Word says and it is the equivalent to not receiving the provision made for us at the cross.

The nature of God's forgiveness is that you are *not* guilty. If you are not guilty, there is no more reason to be ashamed. If Jesus has saved you from your sins, that includes the effect of your sins. The main effect of sin is guilt. The worst thing about sin is how it breaks your capacity to fellowship with God. Nothing is more traumatic than how sin makes you feel inside and that is because it makes you feel alienated, rejected, and separated from God. But through the blood sacrifice of Jesus, not only are our sins taken away, but we can now connect with God intimately. We can have a clear conscience and supreme peace.

You can be free from the effects of shame. Don't live with or have shame any longer. I wrote this book to expose it because it lurks inside your mind. It wants to hang on and continue to impact you. But today, as you read this book, God is saying *no more shame*. This is something you *do not* have to live with. This has gone on entirely too long. It is time for shame to end.

One of the striking elements in our focal scripture Isaiah 61:7, is the reference to **YOUR SHAME**. The exegetical interpretation easily shifts in that this is not just something the Children of Israel experienced over 2000 years ago but it is quite applicable to us today. The cause for the discussion of shame is relevant. There are no punches being pulled. Isaiah is straight to the point about it being your shame. It is something that you possess as your own. Isaiah calls it something that you have taken ownership of. It is particular to you, a part of who you are as an individual. Something happened to you and it changed you. It is how shame has now branded you. You are carrying the damage of what happened to you in the form of shame. This goes to your identity. This goes to how you are perceived by others and more importantly, how you view yourself. Shame can become internalized in you to where it no longer is something separate from you. It belongs to you. It is you.

The consequences of unaddressed shame can be very detrimental. Whenever, the causes of shame are not properly dealt with, the effect on your personhood will be impacted in a negative way. We must stop pretending, lying, and faking like everything is alright, when indeed it is not. I have talked to so many precious people who said they allowed things to go too far. Before they realized it their thoughts were very toxic. They were suffering with depression, hate, bitterness, and thoughts of suicide.

It is much more problematic when you need to remove something that is a part of you. It is one thing to take away something that is foreign or added on but when something is a part of you, it is much more serious. Isaiah is referring to how shame affects how you think and what you think about. Shame becomes a part of how you relate to others and especially to God. Shame dampens your optimism. It weakens your confidence. It causes you to anticipate rejection and worst of all it inhibits your faith. Every time you attempt to do something, there is a voice inside you that says don't you get embarrassed again. There is this fear existing in your memory bank that raises its voice every time you face challenges. Saying things like, "Remember what happened before." or "Do you really fit in?" It is your shame. This way of thinking must be reversed. Somehow you need relief from this limiting and painful part of you.

Shame has become the root of many emotions, and the cause for many behaviors. Shame is motivating certain fears and anxiety. It has become intertwined in your mind in a way where it is influencing how you process things. God desires for us to see or realize the root cause of situations in our lives, so He always goes to the root of things. Deliverance is never just on the surface. God is not merely into trimming the branches; God goes right to the source, the origin, and the root of bondage. Therefore, Isaiah is saying that because of your shame and confusion, you shall have a double portion of joy.

God will remove the shame and give you something better in return. The shame will not continue to be a part of your experience. God will do away with it. He will end its reign in your life. There is to be a separation of this awful scourge that has afflicted you for too long. This evil you have owned for so long is about to be disconnected from you. He wants to break the power of shame over you. He wants you to be liberated and freed from it. The good news is that nothing you have experienced is beyond God's ability to help you. Absolutely nothing!

You, however, have a role too. Your role is to believe God's Word. I, personally, have found that the more I began to believe God's Word regarding the shame in my life its tight reign began to loosen. Once I realized I could have a better life, free from shame, I made it a priority to study, read, write, meditate, quote as much of the Word as possible so that it would resonate in my spirit. There is power in the Word! I was not only able to change the way I believed toward the Word of God but my trust in God flourished. Philippians 4:8 became a litmus test for me. "...Whatsoever things are true, whatsoever things are honest, whatsoever things are just, whatsoever things are pure, whatsoever things are lovely, whatsoever things are of good report; if there be any virtue, and if there be any praise, think on these things." Your shame which has been a part of your personality, a part of your way of thinking must be severed from you. You must legally take measures to divorce yourself from this former partner of yours. Accepting God's Word is rejecting the false premise of bondage. Shame has existed. It has been allowed to become so entrenched because you believed something that is not true. It is God's truth that must and will set you free. You must believe the truth to experience relief from shame. Jesus said, "Ye shall know the truth and the truth shall set you free." (John 8:32). The false narrative you were led to believe is the reason shame existed in your life. Deliverance is not merely God taking shame away, but deliverance also results when you believe and take God at His Word. God's Word discredits the lie and supports the basis for your liberation from shame. Changing the narrative allows you to change your life. When you believe the true nature of what has happened in your life, freedom becomes possible.

A lot of things you assumed about yourself can change when you believe the truth. Shame is one thing you simply do not need to live under anymore. The limits you have been under and the bondage you have had to endure is no longer necessary when you discover the truth about your past. Just like fear, shame is based on lies. It is based on a false narrative. It is stuff you've been led to believe that were true but are in fact, false. For example, the children of Israel *read more into the Babylonian captivity* than was true. They assumed that because they were conquered by the Babylonians and taken into captivity that God had forsaken them. They assumed this meant they were no longer God's people.

They assumed God would no longer use them. They assumed because God punished them for their sin, He had rejected them as His people. They thought they were no longer the apple of His eye. They thought He no longer had His favor over them. But all of that was not true. Shame was based on them exaggerating the meaning of this captivity. Because of their negative thinking they became miserable and assumed the worst about themselves. Isaiah is reassuring them that God had not forsaken them. He was not giving up on them. It was a false narrative. All of this is a testament to God's love and commitment to them. While other nations went into oblivion after something like this happened, God had kept them. The true narrative points to the faithfulness and provisions of God. They did have a future. There was nothing to be ashamed of. They could hold their head up. Despite the extreme nature of their loss, God was ready to give them back double. Instead of feeling as if all was loss, they had a lot to look forward to.

Are there things that happened in your life you believe were your downfall? Are you thinking there are things that people did to you that messed you up? Can you think of things that traumatized you and because of those things you can only go so far? I want to suggest to you those things are all false narratives. I want to tell you that when you believe a false narrative you allow shame to continue to rule over your life. The true narrative is that despite what you did, or what people did and despite what happened, God preserved you. He has great plans for you. Jeremiah 29:11, "For I know the thoughts that I think toward you, saith the Lord, thoughts of peace, and not of evil, to give you an expected end." You see, He wants to use those very things to be the benchmark for you to see just how much He loves you and will bless you.

For your shame you shall receive double blessings. God is doing more than just enough; He is giving you double. How does He address the shame? He addresses the shame by blessing you in a way where you adopt a positive perception and a new perspective. He deals with each person in a unique way because shame's influence on each person varies. With that being said, the first layer to be addressed for many is the victim mindset that shame leads with the person is: **You are the only one. I say to you, you are not!** What has always been interpreted as a mistake or tragedy can be a source of empowerment to help others. The enemy meant it for destruction.

God sees it as an opportunity for construction. You can look back with gratefulness. You can look back and feel good about your journey. Mistakes were made but you are in no way a mistake. It is critical that you replace every lie with a corresponding Word of God (Truth).

It begins with you disowning shame. Shame is no longer true about you. You are not that shameful person you thought you were all those years. You were lied to. You were tricked. You were led to believe something that is flat out not true. The reality of God's Word changes your identity. You are not the person you thought you were. You are not a reject because you were rejected by people. You are not a failure because things failed in your life. You are not a loser because you suffered loss. All of these are false narratives. The truth is God has shown His tremendous love toward you; despite those things having happened, He can still edify you and He can still be glorified in your life. You are a testimony to God's preserving power. You are the perfect candidate to receive and experience God's faithfulness and His blessings of deliverance, healing, and restoration. You can expect double for your trouble. As a result of what you went through, you are about to receive double!

I want you to decide that God's Word is true. That these false narratives you initially believed that caused you to live with shame –they are false. I want you to decide that you will believe, about yourself, what God's Word says is true about you. You must decide and be determined to make a quality decision that you are not going be a person with shame. Shame is no longer applicable to you. Shame has controlled you too long. It is time to realize shame is not your identity. It is time to separate this force on the inside of you from the real you. You have a new name. You have a new identity. You are a new creation in Christ. Shame cannot go along anymore because it is not compatible with who you are. You must own your new identity in Christ. When you realize you are free, shame can no longer occupy any places in your life.

QUESTION FOR YOU:

Who are YOU, really?

_____

_____

_____

_____

_____

_____

_____

_____

_____

_____

_____

_____

JOURNALING MY THOUGHTS

CHAPTER FOUR

Rehashing, Revisiting, Repenting and
Rewriting

In many miracles Jesus performed, there was a command given after the person received their deliverance. Jesus understood there was a need for the person to adopt a new way of being or living to remain delivered. There was an entire set of behaviors and coping mechanisms associated with their affliction. Now that the affliction was gone, it was necessary to do things differently. In Mark 5:18, 19, the delivered man wants to go with Jesus, however, Jesus did not permit him, but said to him, "Go home to your friends, and tell them what great things the Lord has done for you, and how He has had compassion on you." Sharing his testimony would keep him conscious of God's deliverance in his life and prevent him from reverting to the ways when he was bound. The root cause of his problem was an obsession with himself. He spent all day and night thinking only about himself. Jesus had him to do something that kept him from reverting to that old pattern. Instead, Jesus had him to think about how good God had been to him.

Or what about when Jesus told the man by the pool to rise, take up his bed and walk. John 5:8-9a, "Jesus said to him, "Rise, take up your bed and walk." And immediately the man was made well, took up his bed, and walked:" Clearly the significance of this was that he would carry his bed because he couldn't get back in it if he is carrying it. This man was used to having someone help him. He was instructed to do something which made him take responsibility for himself. This kept him from sinking back into the rut of thinking he needed to lay in that bed as he had done for 38 years.

A lot of ministry took place after individuals were delivered. He told the woman with the issue of blood to go in peace because her faith had saved her. See, Mark 5:34 (Message) Jesus said to her, "...Daughter, you took a risk of faith, and now you're healed and whole. Live well, live blessed! Be healed of your plague." Once you are delivered the inner turmoil associated with these traumatic experiences can end. You can now go in peace.

I want to talk to you about some things you can do to ensure shame is gone forever. Once you are delivered from the root of shame, now there is the work of eradicating the effects of its existence in your life. Even though shame is gone, your mind must be changed in the way you think. You must learn how to live without shame. Sometimes there are many things you assumed about yourself that were not true about you. Those things were really the effects of shame. Shame made you a specific way. Shame is why you reacted to situations the way you did. Shame caused you to favor certain kinds of things. Shame could have been behind the relationships you sought. But when shame is removed, suddenly all these things can be different. You no longer need to compensate for having shame; you can live life without the negative effect of shame.

I want to suggest to you a four-step process of ridding shame from your life, forever. Four things need to be done. There needs to be a **rehashing, a revisiting, repenting, and rewriting.**

To rehash is to speak differently.

To revisit is to see things differently.

To repent is to do things differently.

To rewrite is to have a new narrative.

First, we must **rehash.** What you say out of your

mouth is critical to your deliverance. It is necessary to speak God's Word. True freedom is to boldly decree and declare God's Word out loud. Shame influences what you say and how you say things. When thinking has shame in it, it comes out in what you say. What you say out of your mouth reinforces the shame you were thinking. As a matter of fact, much of what you say is filtered through a shame mindset. Ending the thinking of shame involves changing what you say about shame. No one has greater influence on what you think then you. Your mind listens to what you say more so than anyone else in this world. The best way to deprogram yourself from shame and program yourself without shame is to speak the right words out of your mouth. Don't spend the rest of your life rehashing why this, that, or the other happened. When you allow God to heal your mindset, the effect is who you were really meant to be comes to the forefront. Your life will become more fulfilling. John 10:10, "The thief cometh not, but for to steal, and to kill, and to destroy: I am come that they might have life, and that they might have it more abundantly."

Sometimes Jesus would have people speak specific words distinctly to get them to say the right words. Having them say the appropriate words allowed them to hear correctly so that their mindset could be changed. Jesus asked questions that caused people to say things they could hear for themselves. Although Jesus knew everything, the reason He asked them questions was not to get information from them, but to get them to hear the words from their mouths. When they heard it from their own mouths it would change what they were thinking about their situation.

You must recognize the power of what you say out of your mouth. I need you to say things true about yourself according to the Word of God. There must be a reinforcement of God's Word so that there is no place for shame to ever return. In this way, you are so occupied with saying the truth that there is no opportunity to say anything that would evoke shame.

I dare say you may find that you have an entirely new skill set now that shame is gone. You may even take on a different personality now that shame is no longer influencing you. I believe you might become a different person when you no longer need to deal with the scourge of shame.

Then, there must be a change in your thinking regarding your past. This involves the need to **revisit** the occurrence of shame from your past. The way you view things that happened in your past has a great bearing on how you view things in the present. Those things also affect how you view things in the future. Shame is centered in your memory bank. It appeared at some point and has lived in your subconscious. When you get delivered, the mind is

71

accustomed to thinking a certain way. You must reprogram your mind. "And do not be conformed to this world, but be transformed by the renewing of your mind, that you may prove what is that good and acceptable and perfect will of God." (Romans 12:2, NKJV). It is imperative that you change your normal default. You need to challenge certain common assumptions in you because of shame and assume different things that reflect the fact that you are now free from shame.

A change in your thinking starts with a change in your thoughts. The first step is to manage what you think. There needs to be a conscious effort to reverse the course of your thinking caused by shame. It starts in how you view your past. That is, the things you are ashamed of or caused you to feel shame must be perceived differently in your mind. They have been a source of pain and regret but now they need to be revisited with the Truth which is the Word of

God. These things should be viewed no longer as tragedies or failures but examples of God's grace and mercy. You must change your perspective. The hurt and the brokenness were definitely real. However, you are still alive. Get Up! There are lives hanging in the balance in need of your story. So, when you **revisit with the TRUTH** of God's Word, shame is no match.

Next, there is a need to **repent**. Meaning there is a need to do things differently. To reinforce your deliverance, you may even have to do things you have never done before. Deliverance can be wrought by the sheer action that defies the control of the bondage over your life. There were many instances in the Bible where God commanded people to do something, which was a way to bring about their deliverance *from* something. The lepers were cleansed as they obeyed Jesus' command to show themselves to the priest. (Luke 17:11-19). The blind man was able to see when he washed in the pool of Siloam. (John 9:7).

I believe that is why God moves in particular ways in our lives. He chooses ways that challenge our way of thinking. His goal is to make sure the chaff will not continue to impose upon our lives. There are things we learn from doing those things that free us inside. Requiring the children of Israel to dispossess the Canaanites from the land was a way to change them from a slave mentality to having a conquering mentality. You need to go toward your fears. Shame made you stay within a specific boundary. Now that you are free, it is time to step outside your own shame-imposed barriers. It is time to do what you never thought you could do. God will give you opportunities to display your new-found freedom. Repentance is a change in your ways. It is a change in what you do.

Last but certainly not least, there is a need to

rewrite your story. Write new and positive narratives that will make these experiences provoke praise as opposed to things that cause you to feel shame. God wants to use the very experience shame used to keep you down, to be the very reason for which you now rejoice. He wants your testing to become a testimony. He wants your greatest failures to point to God's miraculous victories in your life. Despite all that went wrong, God wants to bless you double for your trouble.

I got married in 1982. My husband was a minister. Apparently, many folks felt that since I was married to a minister, I should have a whole bunch of children immediately. When that didn't transpire, they came up with their own shameful assessments aimed at me! "She thinks she is cute, she don't want to lose her shape, she infertile". It was all about what I was not doing. The Pastor was excused! Little did they know that we were told we couldn't have children? As we sat in the doctor's office THAT DAY I turned to my husband and said, "Am I barren?" While this was the reality for both my husband and I, I could not help but take responsibility. It had to be my fault because he already had a daughter. However, I just couldn't accept that diagnosis because the Holy Spirit had already told me my womb was blessed early within my marriage. Despite the report from the doctor, it took everything in me to stand on the Word I received from God. I would even continue to believe God when I conceived in 1992 and miscarried. In 1994 at the tender age of 36 Danielle Sabrina was born (natural childbirth) and in 1998 at the age of 40 (age is only a number). I received my double for my troubles blessing with the birth of Diamond Shekinah (natural childbirth too)!

From now on, whenever you think about something that used to be the basis for shame, I want you to think about how God used it to raise you up.

He used that situation to reveal to you just how real He could be in your life. You see, He used evil to bring about so much good. Romans 8:28, "And we know that all things work together for good to them that love God, to them who are the called according to his purpose."

It is critical that you embrace what Jesus did for you on the cross. Jesus has erased everything from your past; therefore, you don't have to live with shame. He has already made provisions for you to have a new identity free from shame. No matter what the unfortunate experiences were or what happened in the past, they are covered by the blood of Jesus. The debt has been paid in full. There is no need for you to make any more payments or restitutions. You have been justified, which literally means just as if you never sinned. The only way shame can come back is if you stop believing in all Jesus did for you. The cleansing was an important part of the Old

Testament sacrificial system. The death of animals was one aspect of the atonement, but the other part was to sprinkle the blood which symbolized the cleansing from the effect of the sin. Jesus sprinkled His precious blood on the mercy seat to cleanse us from our sins.

Which is why John tells us we must confess our sins so we can be forgiven, but then the additional step is that we might be cleansed from all unrighteousness? In 1 John 1:9, "...If we confess our sins, he is faithful and just to forgive us our sins, and to cleanse us from all unrighteousness." There is an additional work of being cleansed. This is the removal of our shame mindset. The after effect of having been bound by shame must be addressed. The mind must be cleansed and purged from the evil thinking associated with shame. Any time shame tries to enter your mind you have to reject it outright. You must claim the finished work of Jesus Christ on the cross and know that you have been freed from shame.

It is time for praise to replace pity. It is time for worship to replace worry. Instead of regret think about the goodness He has shown toward you. We are talking about a changed mindset. You now have a different way of thinking. You can now have a new perspective.

I want you to fill your mind with thoughts of victory, joy, and love. You can think victoriously because you have overcome shame. Now, consider yourself an over comer. You can think joyfully because you can rejoice in your newfound freedom. You can move forward with confidence knowing God has accepted you in the Beloved! (Ephesians 1:6)

Journaling My Thoughts

CHAPTER FIVE

Walking in Your Deliverance from Shame

I need you to engage in an exercise that will initiate a transformation from shame to glory. Now that we have laid out the problem of shame, it is now time to experience deliverance. Everything up to this point has been to bring you to this place of change. The truths you have been exposed to in this book have set you up to receive an explosion of power that will literally compel or make you a new person. While I cannot be there personally in this moment, I have prayed that you will sense the presence of the Holy Spirit who is ready to do something miraculous in your life right now. The way this is going to transpire is by you simply speaking forth God's Word. As you speak the things below truth will replace the false and evil basis for all the shame in your life. As Jesus said, ye shall know the truth and the truth will make you free. (John 8:32) Words are the medium of exchange in the Spirit realm. Words carry power and can transmit spiritual life to your heart. There is a divine transaction that can take place right now inside you in which you can experience complete relief from your years of being in bondage to shame. As you have believed in your heart now it is time to confess with your mouth. The truths you have believed can now be manifested as you speak it out of your mouth. You are literally reprogramming your mind. You are planting the appropriate assumptions in your heart. These words that you will speak will travel deep down on the inside of you to the critical areas where shame has been entrenched. You will literally cast down imaginations, and every high thing that exalteth itself against the knowledge of God, and you will bring into captivity every thought to the obedience of Christ. (See, 2 Corinthians 10:5) This will begin is a change on the inside of you that will not only rid you of shame but set you on the course where shame has no more place in your life. I am talking about a change in your overall pattern of thinking. A change in your perspective, which will lead to a new fresh way to perceive reality, is what is about to happen. The words listed below are the suggested adjectives describing what you must say, not just for today, but for anytime the enemy tries to bring shame back up in your life. This is your declaration of *your* independence! I need you to say these words over yourself. For example, "I Sabrina Antoinette Jefferson Lloyd Mangrum, now relish in the truth that I am Chosen! I declare and I say what God says about me." Being chosen was not the only truth God said about me. He spoke many other liberating attributes to me as well. The following pages lists some of my life changing attributes. What does God say about You? Herein at the end of this Chapter, you will have the opportunity to list your attributes.

QUESTION FOR YOU:

What are the attributes God has spoken over you?

_____

_____

_____

_____

_____

_____

_____

_____

_____

_____

_____

_____

This list is not exhaustive; you may adapt, where applicable.

Powerful. I am powerful. First, I need you to say you are powerful. That means you are capable, strong, energetic, and vigorous. You have the ability and the readied skill to apply to any situation in which to have a favorable outcome. Philippians 4:13 says, "I can do all things through Christ which strengtheneth me."

Loved. I am loved. I need you to say you are loved. This means you are valued; you are desirable; you are important; and you are treasured. You are accepted and considered precious. Song of Solomon 6:3a says, "I am my beloved's, and my beloved is mine:…"

Bold. I am bold. I need you to speak over yourself that you are bold. That means you are daring, enterprising and willing to take risks. You are equipped with holy boldness. You have great courage and you are fearless.

Proverbs 28:1 says, "The wicked flee when no man pursueth: but the righteous are bold as a lion."

Victorious. I am victorious. I need you make a confession that you are victorious. That means you are a champion. You are a winner in any contest or struggle. You are triumphant over anything you face. There is an enduring quality about you where you never allow yourself to lose.

2 Corinthians 2:14 says; "Now thanks be unto God, which always causeth us to triumph in Christ..."

Intelligent. I am intelligent. I need you to hear yourself say that you are intelligent. That means you are brilliant, knowledgeable, and smart. You have the ability, to apply applicable reason and wisdom to any situation. You have discretion and excellent judgement in decision making. You are circumspect (cautious) and have keen foresight. Proverbs 18:4 says, "The words of a man's mouth are as deep waters, and the wellspring of wisdom as a flowing brook."

Confident. I am confident. You must see yourself as being confident, meaning you are assured and have an absolute certainty about yourself. That means you have belief in what you can do. You now trust in yourself. You carry yourself in a way where there is an air of conviction and certitude (certainty) about what you can do.

Free. I am free. Declaring yourself free might be the most important thing you say out of your mouth. That means you reject any inhibition, restriction, or limitation about yourself or any external source. This is a release for you from feeling the need to meet other people's expectations or the need to obtain outside approval from others. You say to yourself that God's affirmation is all you need. You will only operate in the freedom Christ has given you in Him. Galatians 5:1 says, "Stand fast therefore in the liberty wherewith Christ hath made us free and be not entangled again with the yoke of bondage."

Purpose. I need you to see yourself as having meaning and fulfilling a divine purpose. To attest within yourself that you are intentional and resolved to make a major impact in the lives of others is what must come out of your mouth. You must see your life as making a difference in this world. You are appointed to leave a legacy of greatness to future generations. Jeremiah 29:11, "For I know the thoughts that I think toward you, saith the Lord, thoughts of peace, and not of evil, to give you an expected end."

Equipped. I am equipped. I need you to say you are equipped. I realize there may be some overlap with being confident but being equipped takes it further than merely being confident. To be equipped is to realize how many talents and gifts you possess. It is to appreciate all the lessons you have learned from the experience you have had. It is about drawing upon how the trials have developed you and trained you to operate at a high level of performance. "But I have prayed for thee, that thy faith fail not: and when thou art converted, strengthen thy brethren." (Luke 22:32)

Favored. The last thing I want you to say is that you are favored. That means you are special and chosen. Not only are you not to operate with shame but you are to speak of yourself in high regard. Without being arrogant or prideful, you speak of yourself as God sees you –as the apple of His eye. You see yourself as being unique and singled-out for your significance. Psalms 139:17-18 says, "How precious also are thy thoughts unto me, O God! how great is the sum of them! If I should count them, they are more in number than the sand: when I awake, I am still with thee."

If I should count them, they are more in number than the sand: when I awake, I am still with thee."

No more shame!

I want it gone—all gone!

Journaling My Thoughts

PRAYER

Dear Jesus, I ask you to deliver and heal me today.

I've been bullied by shame far too long.

I ask You to free me from public shame.

I ask You to free me from private shame.

Today, I receive Your unconditional love for me.

Thank You for exposing shame and its repercussions if I

allow it to remain in my life.

I believe by faith that I am free.

It is time for me to move forward with my life in You.

Romans 10:9-10

I boldly decree and declare an Isaiah 61:7 mindset.

I move FORWARD with great expectation and Joy!

I AM FREE

In Jesus' Name, AMEN!

ABOUT THE AUTHOR

Pastor Sabrina A. Mangrum is a motivational speaker, executive coach, and founder and CEO of W.O.R.D. Women of Rare Distinction®. W.O.R.D. is a women's ministry with local, national and international impact, equipping women to live their best lives for Christ at home, in their community and in the marketplace.

Her passion for people hurting and struggling under the weight of past trauma and emotional pain has led her down many ministerial paths. So many have been freed and delivered through her powerful ministry. Whether ministering at church, a conference or an intimate coaching session, her message is the same: you can experience the abundant life by accessing the unlimited resources of God's Word.

She was licensed to preach the Gospel in July 1985 and ordained in September 1993. She graduated from Howard University's School of Divinity in Washington, DC, with a Master of Divinity degree. She is a recipient of the Nannie Helen Burroughs 2019 Award in Pastoral Leadership. She received her Bachelor's degree in Business Administration from the University of Maryland, College Park.

Pastor Sabrina views herself as a servant of the Most High God, and gives Him all the praise, glory and honor for her life. She is married to Daniel T. Mangrum, and from this union they have two brilliant, beautiful and accomplished daughters, Danielle Sabrina and Diamond Shekinah.

9 781734 675832